abcdefghijklmn

abbreviation

An abbreviat
word or a grc

> Dr (Doctor), NHS (National Health Service), LEA (Local Education Authority), Ltd (Limited)

acronym

This is an abbreviation made up of the first letters of a group of words, pronounced as one word.

> NATO (North Atlantic Treaty Organisation)
> RAM (Random Access Memory)

adjective

An adjective is a word that describes somebody or something.

The adjective may come before or after the noun.

> The **strange, little** dog with the **long** tail
> The **red** dress
> The dress was **red**.

adverb

An adverb is a word or phrase which gives more information about a verb, an adjective, another adverb or a whole sentence. An adverb often tells how, when or where something is done. They often end in -ly.

Please come **here**.

She speaks **quickly** and **quietly**.

alliteration

This is a group of words that begin with the same sound.

Several silent slithering snakes

antonym

A word which means the opposite of another word is an antonym.

Many words have more than one antonym.

hot – cold

big – small / tiny / little

apostrophe

An apostrophe is a punctuation mark (') that is used to show ownership or to show that a word has been shortened by missing out letters.

Sameea's book, the **doctors'** surgery,

the **girl's** coat, the **children's** playground,

I'm afraid there **aren't** any tea-bags left.

auto-biography

A life story written by that person is an autobiography.

Long Walk to Freedom, Nelson Mandela

abcdefghijklmnopqrstuvwxyz

abcdefghijklmnopqrstuvwxyz

abcdefghijklmnopqrstuvwxyz

ballad

A ballad is a poem or song that tells a story.

Frankie and Johnny were sweethearts

bibliography

A list of books or articles is a bibliography.

biography

A biography is the life story of a person, written by someone else.

Posh and Becks, Andrew Morton

abcdefghijklmnopqrstuvwxyz

chronological writing — This is writing that describes events in the order in which they took place.

> many historical accounts, police reports

cliché — A cliché is a word or phrase that has been used so often it loses its impact.

> As sick as a parrot
>
> At this moment in time
>
> We'll leave no stone unturned.

comma — A comma is a punctuation mark (,) used to help the reader by separating parts of a sentence.

> I swear I will tell the truth, the whole truth, and nothing but the truth.

connective

Words and phrases which are used to link parts of a text are connectives. They may be used to make two or more simple sentences into one compound sentence. They may also be used to connect sentences or ideas in a paragraph.

> **but, although, while, if, so that**
>
> I chose red **because** it's my favourite colour.
>
> He loaded the washing machine **before** he started watching television.

consonant

All the letters of the alphabet except the vowels are consonants.

'Y' can act as either a vowel or a consonant.

> b c d f g h j k l m n p q r s t v w x y z
>
> 'y' in 'yes', 'you', 'yellow'

dialogue This is a written or spoken conversation between two people.

discussion This is a text type that presents arguments and information from different points of view.

Arguments for and against a town bypass

abcdefghijklmnopqrstuvwxyz

etymology

Etymology is the study of the origin and history of words.

bi (Latin meaning two): bilingual, bifocals, bicycle

centum (Latin meaning 100): century, centurion, cent, percentage

scribere (Latin meaning to write): script, inscription, scribe

phobos (Greek meaning fear): phobia, agoraphobia

demos (Greek meaning people): democratic

The name for the drink Punch comes from the Hindi word for five. The five ingredients were spirit, water, lemon-juice, sugar and spice.

exclamation mark

This is a punctuation mark (!) used at the end of a sentence to show a strong feeling or emotion like surprise, joy, pain or anger.

Stop! Oh! Fire!

. *The Cambridge Encyclopaedia of the English Language*, David Crystal, Cambridge University Press 1995

explanation

This is a text type that explains how or why something happens or how it works.

The life cycle of a butterfly

How different vehicles work

abcdefghijklmnopqrstuvwxyz

abcdefghijklmnopqrstuvwxyz

fiction

A text in which what happens has been invented by the writer is fiction.

novels, TV dramas, short stories

footnote

Additional information printed at the bottom of the page is a footnote.

See E

abcdefghijklmnopqrstuvwxyz

abcdefghijklmnopqrstuvwxyz

genre

These are different types of writing, each with its own specific characteristics.

science-fiction, historical novels, myth, biography, diary

glossary

A glossary is a list of words or terms and their definitions.

Key Words – Literacy

abcdefghijklmnopqrstuvwxyz

homophone Words which sound the same but have a different meaning are homophones.

pair / pear	right / write	meet / meat
which / witch	road/rowed	

hyphen A hyphen is a punctuation mark (-) used to join two words or to divide a word that runs over from one line to the next.

a German - English dictionary

idiom, idiomatic language

This is an expression that does not make sense if you take the individual words literally.

You look a **bit under the weather** today.

That will **cut no ice** with the manager.

That name **rings a bell**. I know I have heard it somewhere.

I'll have to ask **my better half.**

instruction

This is a text type that aims to help the reader complete a task or achieve a goal.

Recipes

Instructions on playing a board game

How to put furniture together

Jargon

Specialised language used by particular groups (sometimes to exclude others) is called jargon.

> downsizing, rightsizing, dehiring

abcdefghijklmnopqrstuvwxyz

legend

This is a traditional story about heroic characters.

King Arthur and the Knights of the Round Table

Robin Hood

abcdefghijklmnopqrstuvwxyz

meta-language

Language we use to describe how language works is called metalanguage.

sentence, noun, paragraph

mnemonic

A mnemonic is a catchphrase or way of remembering difficult spellings.

Wed**nes**day

There's a rat in **separate**.

One collar two sleeves – **necessary**

Stationery or stationary? There's an e in envelopes.

monologue

This is a text spoken by just one person (unlike a dialogue where there are two people speaking).

morpheme A morpheme is the smallest unit of meaning. A word can be one morpheme, two morphemes, three morphemes.

house – one morpheme

house/s – two morphemes

house/keep/ing – three morphemes

myth A myth is an ancient traditional story.

Romulus and Remus

Daedalus and Icarus

abcdefghijklmnopqrstuvwxyz

narrative

This is a text that re-tells events, often in chronological order.

non-chronological report

This is a text type that describes the way things are without referring to a time sequence.

> a guidebook

non-fiction

Different texts based on facts are known as non-fiction.

> recount, non-chronological report, instruction, explanation, persuasion, discussion

noun

A noun is a word that names something or somebody.

A proper noun is a specific name and starts with a capital letter.

> man, shop, town, street
>
> **J**im, **W**oolworth, **L**eicester, **S**tation **R**oad.

onomato-poeia

Onomatopoeia means words in which the sound echoes the meaning.

hiss, crash, cuckoo

onset

The onset is the initial consonant or consonant cluster of a word.

Some words have no onset.

club, **t**rain, **p**an, **s**un
'Use' and 'out' have no onset.

paragraph — A paragraph is a section of a piece of writing. Each paragraph begins on a new line. It marks a change of focus e.g. time, place, new character speaking.

parable — This is a short story with a moral.

> The story of the Good Samaritan

persuasion — This is a text type that aims to persuade the reader.

> healthy eating leaflet, advertisements

phoneme — The smallest unit of sound in a word is a phoneme. It may be represented by 1, 2, 3 or 4 letters.

> **to**, sh**oe**, cr**ew**, thr**ough**

prefix

A prefix is a morpheme added to the beginning of a word to change its meaning.

> **un**happy, **dis**approve, **anti**freeze, **mis**understand, **pre**school

pronoun

A pronoun is a word used in place of a noun.

> He, him, mine, it

question mark

A punctuation mark (?) which is used at the end of a sentence to show that it is a question, is called a question mark.

It helps the reader to know how to read the text with the correct expression.

> Where do you live?
>
> You live in Leicester?

abcdefghijklmnopqrstuvwxyz

recount

This is a text type that retells events in the order that they took place.

a newspaper report, a biography

rime

The rime is the part of a syllable which contains the vowel and final consonant/s.

c**at**,	t**orn**,	f**eel**,	th**atch**,	spl**ash**

sentence

A sentence is a group of words that makes sense by itself.

Sentences start with a capital letter, end with a full stop and contain a verb.

> The dog bit him.
>
> The entire village was ruined by the hurricane and people had no shelter for many days.
>
> Would you like coffee or tea?

skim

This is a way of reading to get a quick first impression of the meaning.

suffix

A morpheme added to the end of a word is the suffix.

> talk**ing**, amuse**ment**, slow**ly**, tree**s**, work**ed**

syllable

A syllable is each beat in a word.

Every syllable contains a vowel.

cat (1 syllable), catkin (2),
catapult (3), caterpillar (4)

synopsis

A brief summary of the main points in a book or an article is called a synopsis.

synonym

Synonyms are words which have the same or similar meanings.

wet / damp — easy / simple
true / right / correct / accurate / certain

text types

Text types are different kinds of writing.

discussion, explanation, instruction, fiction, narrative, non-chronological report, non-fiction, recount, persuasion

thesaurus

A thesaurus is a reference book that lists alternative words with similar meanings.

fast, swift, quick, rapid, hasty, speedy

verb

A verb is a word or group of words which names an action, a happening, a process or state of being.

do, go, eat,
have done, is going, will eat

vowel

There are 5 vowels.

'Y' can act as either a vowel or a consonant.

a, e, i, o, u
'y' in 'happy', 'fly'

writing frame

A structured outline to support different kinds of writing is called a writing frame.

A framework to complete a letter or CV

Opening phrases for a story to be continued by the writer

abcdefghijklmnopqrstuvwxy**z**